AMAZING HISTORY

SHIPWRECKS

JAMES STEWART

A+

Smart Apple Media

Published by Smart Apple Media
2140 Howard Drive West
North Mankato, MN 56003

Created by Q2A Media
Series Editor: Jean Coppendale
Designers: Diksha Khatri, Ashita Murgai
Picture Researchers: Lalit Dalal, Jyoti Sachdev
Illustrators: Hemant Arya, Manish Prasad, Amir Khan

Printed in China

The Library of Congress has cataloged the hardcover edition as follows:

Stewart, James, 1950–
Shipwrecks / by James Stewart.
p. cm. — (Amazing history)
Includes index.
ISBN 978-1-59920-105-4 (hardcover)
ISBN 978-1-59920-206-8 (pbk)
1. Shipwrecks—Juvenile literature. I. Title.

G525.S8814 2007
910.4'52—dc22   2007021699

First Edition

9 8 7 6 5 4 3 2 1

Contents

Why do ships sink?

When the sea rages, ships can be seriously damaged or wrecked. But shipwrecks can be caused by many other things, such as an explosion on board or a sudden leak, a **collision** or **running aground**, a fire or an error of **navigation**.

Explosion

On February 15, 1898, the United States **battleship** *Maine* was tied up in Havana **harbor** in Cuba when it suddenly exploded. This shipwreck helped spark the Spanish-American war. Later, the ship's own **gunpowder** was found to have exploded by accident.

HOT SPOTS

In 2002, two ships, the Tricolor *and* the Kariba, *collided in the English Channel. The Tricolor sank with 2,862 luxury cars on board.*

The explosion of the U.S. battleship *Maine*, which killed 260 men.

The wreckage of the Chinese gunboat *Tien Sing*, on St. John's Reef, in the Red Sea. Because of a navigational error the ship's bottom was ripped out on the dangerous reef.

On the rocks

The SS *Princess May* hit a **reef** close to Alaska's Sentinel Island on August 5, 1910, in full view of the **lighthouse**. As the tide went out, the ship stayed perched dangerously on the jagged rocks. All 80 passengers and 68 **crew** members were rescued.

The *Princess May* was trapped on the rocks for almost a month. The ship was pulled free by tug boats.

Up in the air!
People waiting to be rescued

The *Mary Rose*

Shipwrecks do not always happen in storms. Sometimes sailors or shipbuilders make a mistake and a ship sinks in calm weather. This is what happened to the *Mary Rose*.

Pride of a king

The *Mary Rose* was English King Henry VIII's finest warship. In 1545, after many battles and having been fitted with powerful new guns, it sailed out from Portsmouth harbor to attack the French **fleet**. But before firing a single shot, the ship turned—and sank! The sea had flooded in through the open gun ports, making the ship top-heavy.

United Kingdom

Portsmouth harbor

Mary Rose **wreck**

When the *Mary Rose* sank, most of the crew drowned, including the captain.

BABCOCK POWER CONSTRUCTION DIVISION

T.C.W.I

WULF CUXHAVEN

Up, up, and away
A lifting frame was used to raise the wreck

Strong support
A support cradle protected the fragile wooden remains

The wreck of the *Mary Rose* was finally rescued in 1982. It is now restored and on display in Portsmouth, UK.

Raising the wreck

The *Mary Rose* lay on the seabed for 437 years. It was lifted on October 11, 1982, and work to restore it began in 1994. In 2003 and 2004, parts of the ship's left side were found at the bottom of the sea. These large pieces of wood had probably broken away from the ship when it sank. More than 22,000 valuable items were found on the wreck, including navigation equipment, guns, and board games.

HOT SPOTS

Built between 1509 and 1511, the Mary Rose *was named for King Henry VIII's favorite sister, Mary. The rose was the* **Tudor** *family emblem.*

Treasure ships

When Spain ruled large parts of the **New World**, it used **galleons** to carry treasure, such as gold and silver, across the Atlantic to Europe. But these treasure ships attracted pirates, and their battles led to many shipwrecks.

Pirates and privateers

Pirates were often hired by their home country to rob enemy ships of their treasure. Many pirates, or **privateers** as they were known, came from France and England. One of the most famous was Francis Drake. In 1587, Drake turned from piracy to warfare. He led an English fleet into the Spanish harbor of Cadiz and set fire to many enemy ships.

Francis Drake attacking a Spanish treasure ship.

HOT SPOTS

After sailing around the world in his ship, the Golden Hind, *Francis Drake was knighted by Queen Elizabeth I in 1581.*

The sinking of the SS *Golden Gate*

On July 27, 1862, the SS *Golden Gate* left San Francisco bound for Panama. There were 338 passengers and crew members on board, plus $1.4 million in gold. Tragically, the voyage was never completed. The steamship caught fire and sank off the coast of Manzanillo, Mexico, and more than 200 people died.

Only 100 passengers survived the wreck of the *Golden Gate*.

On the rocks

The ship was driven onto rocks that smashed its **rudder**

The wreck of the *Vrouw Maria* (Virgin Mary), which sank during a storm in 1771, off the coast of Finland. The wooden merchant ship was sailing to St. Petersburg, Russia.

The *Vasa*

In 1626, King Gustavus Adolphus of Sweden ordered a huge warship to be built. Named after his royal house, *Vasa*, he wanted the ship for the war against his neighbor, Poland.

Harbor disaster

At the time, the *Vasa* was the greatest ship ever built. The **hull** was 16 feet (5 m) tall and carried 64 heavy **cannons** made of **brass**. The *Vasa* set sail for the first time on August 10, 1628. As it sailed out of Stockholm harbor, crowds cheered and the ship fired its guns to celebrate. Suddenly, a gust of wind caught the sails. The ship lurched, leaned heavily to one side and stayed there. Ten minutes after leaving port, the *Vasa* sank.

Sweden

Stockholm

Poland

As the *Vasa* started to lean over, sea water flooded through the open gun ports.

Decked out
The *Vasa* had two gun decks instead of one, which made it extra heavy

Great escape
Most of the crew escaped from the sinking *Vasa*

Raising the *Vasa*

The wreck of the *Vasa* was still in good condition when it was found. Attempts to raise it began in 1956 and took five years to complete. After drilling tunnels beneath its **keel**, cables were passed through these tunnels, and the ship was lifted to the surface. While it was still under water, divers repaired the wreck with oak pegs and wooden padded covers. The *Vasa* finally appeared above the water on April 24, 1961.

HOT SPOTS

Many fascinating treasures were found in the wreck of the Vasa, *including the officers' pewter dinner service, bronze candlesticks, barrels of meat, a coat of arms, and silver and bronze coins from the seventeenth century.*

The *Vasa* has now been restored and is on display in a specially built museum in Skansen, Sweden.

Golden carvings

The wooden carvings were painted gold. They showed emperors, knights, lions, monsters, and mermaids

Chinese treasure wrecks

During the fifteenth century, the Chinese traveled great distances in huge ships filled with valuable pottery and silk. Some of these ships were wrecked. They are still being discovered, and their treasures sold to collectors around the world.

The *Royal Nanhai*

In 1994, the wreck of a Chinese junk, the *Royal Nanhai*, was found in the South China Sea, off the coast of Malaysia. Archaeologists think this huge ship broke up in heavy seas around 1460. It was probably taking a **cargo** of valuable **porcelain** from China to Java. About 20 percent of this cargo has been recovered in excellent condition and the most valuable pieces are now in museums around the world.

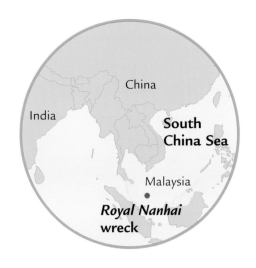

China

India

South China Sea

Malaysia

Royal Nanhai **wreck**

A sketch of the wreck of the *Royal Nanhai* showing porcelain stored below deck.

Precious cargo
Nearly 21,000 pieces of pottery have been recovered

A marine archaeologist cleaning some of the precious porcelain found in the wreck of the *Royal Nanhai*.

HOT SPOTS

Admiral Zheng He was given gifts by the rulers of the many countries he visited. He took back the first zebra, giraffe, ostrich, and oryx to be seen in China.

Early wrecks

Between 1404 and 1433, the government in China organized seven naval expeditions under the command of Admiral Zeng He. On his first voyage, he had 317 ships with more than 27,000 crew. These ships were the largest vessels at the time. The fleets sailed to India, the Persian Gulf, and down the coast of East Africa. Some were wrecked in storms and lie at the bottom of the ocean.

Christopher Columbus's ship, the *Pinta*, is tiny beside one of Zheng He's ships, which were up to 480 feet (146 m) long.

Vast masts

Each treasure ship had nine huge masts

A light in the dark

Lighthouses are built near the sea to mark the coastline in the dark. The first lighthouse, built in 290 B.C., was in Alexandria, Egypt.

Longstone lighthouse

United Kingdom

Eddystone lighthouse

Lights out

In 1703, Henry Winstanley built one of the UK's first lighthouses on the Eddystone Rocks outside Plymouth. He said his wooden building could survive the roughest weather. He was in it when a test came on November 26, 1703. That night, the worst storm ever known hit the UK. The next morning, people went to see if the lighthouse was still there. Horrified, they saw that Winstanley and his building had completely disappeared.

No one can be really sure, but strong winds and the pounding sea probably smashed the Eddystone lighthouse to pieces.

Grace Darling and her father rescued the survivors from a ship wrecked during the night.

Grace Darling with her father and other rescuers at sea

Darling rescue

Grace Darling lived with her father in the Longstone lighthouse, on sharp rocks off the northeast coast of the UK. One September morning in 1838, the Darlings rowed through rough seas to rescue nine people clinging to rocks. Grace became a heroine, and a museum was named after her. Grace and her father were also awarded the Royal National Lifeboat Institution's Silver Medal.

HOT SPOTS

*Today, lighthouses are mechanical, so people no longer need to live in them. Floating **buoys** with lights or bells also warn sailors of dangerous coasts.*

Wreckers!

Rocky coasts are battered by mighty storms that often leave ships torn apart on the rocks. In the past, people living nearby have realized that they could profit from these wrecks. And some say not all of these shipwrecks were accidents.

Free for all

In the dark, captains steered their ships guided by lights on the shore. But what if someone moved a light? It is said that the **wreckers** did this to lead ships toward rocks, so they could steal the cargo. We do not know why the cargo ship *Postillion* ran into the coast of north Cornwall in 1732. But we do know that wreckers quickly stripped the vessel of everything valuable that could be carried away.

Wreckers may have waved fire torches to lead ships to smash against dangerous rocks.

Wreckers taking the cargo of brandy from the grounded *Rosina* off Long Island, New York, in 1871. News of a shipwreck spread quickly among local communities, bringing wreckers to the scene to strip the ship of all its cargo.

The wrecking reef

The **looting** of shipwrecks was a very profitable business around the world. In the United States, it was a major industry from the time of the Spanish treasure ships in the sixteenth century to about 1900. Many ships were grounded on the dangerous reefs around Key West, a small island in the Florida Keys, allowing the locals to loot their cargo.

HOT SPOTS

In the 1800s, Key West, Florida, was one of the richest American cities. Its wealth came mainly from the wreckers. Many ships sank in the dangerous Gulf area around the Keys. However, wreckers were required to save passengers before looting the ships.

The *Titanic*

The most famous shipwreck of all time took place in 1912. The *Titanic*, weighing 48,000 tons, was the largest ship in the world. It was on its first voyage, steaming across the Atlantic Ocean from Southampton to New York.

Unsinkable

The builders of the *Titanic* said their ship was so big and well made that it was "unsinkable." How wrong they were! The night of April 14, was calm and clear. The sea was flat and bright stars twinkled in the cold, clear sky. Most of the 2,200 people on board were having a wonderful time.

UNITED KINGDOM

NORTH AMERICA

Southampton

Titanic sank

New York

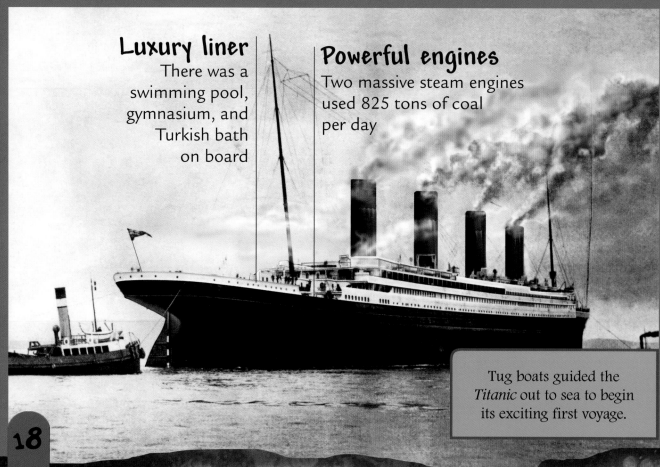

Luxury liner
There was a swimming pool, gymnasium, and Turkish bath on board

Powerful engines
Two massive steam engines used 825 tons of coal per day

Tug boats guided the *Titanic* out to sea to begin its exciting first voyage.

Icy death

Traveling fast in the dark, the *Titanic* suddenly ran into an iceberg. Water poured in through holes ripped in the side. Slowly, over the next two and a half hours, the ship sank into the freezing Atlantic. There were not enough lifeboats for everyone on board, so 1,500 people drowned. Another ship, the *Californian*, was nearby and could have rescued many, but it thought the *Titanic's* signals for help were fireworks!

The law required the *Titanic* to carry only enough lifeboats for half of the passengers and crew on board.

HOT SPOTS

Although six iceberg warnings were given on the day the Titanic *sank, the captain believed there was no need to slow down.*

The wreck of the *Titanic* on the ocean floor. It is covered in barnacles and rust.

19

Wartime shipwrecks

The two world wars were fought as much at sea as on land. Thousands of warships and merchant vessels were wrecked—and tens of thousands of people drowned.

The *Lusitania*

The most famous shipwreck of World War I was probably the SS *Lusitania*, a passenger ship on the way from the U.S. to the UK. On May 7, 1915, a German submarine torpedoed the ship to prevent it from taking supplies to the UK. The huge ship sank in just 18 minutes, drowning 1,198 people.

Secret cargo
The *Lusitania* may have carried a secret cargo of weapons and explosives

The *Lusitania* was hit by a torpedo, which set off a secondary explosion. The U.S. was very angry at the number of Americans killed. Two years later, the U.S. joined the war against Germany.

Pearl Harbor

On December 7, 1941, Japanese warplanes attacked **Pearl Harbor**, Hawaii, where much of the U.S. Pacific fleet was based. The attack destroyed eight American battleships and 188 planes, severely damaged nine other warships, and killed 2,403 American servicemen and 68 **civilians**.

HOT SPOTS

As a result of the attack on Pearl Harbor, President Franklin D. Roosevelt announced that the U.S. was joining World War II against Germany and Japan.

The wrecked destroyers USS *Downes* and USS *Cassin* at the navy yard at Pearl Harbor, shortly after the Japanese attack.

Fire!

Ships catch fire for all sorts of reasons, such as electrical faults on board or an enemy attack. Fire was a major hazard aboard wooden ships. Modern ships carry materials, such as paint and fuel, that also burn easily.

Steam pioneer

USS *Missouri* was the first American warship to cross the Atlantic under steam power, arriving in Gibraltar on August 25, 1843. The following evening, an officer accidentally broke a bottle of turpentine in the storeroom, which quickly caught fire. The flames spread so fast, that in four hours the warship became a blackened, sinking wreck.

Rescue
The British ship *Malabar* rescued about 200 members of the *Missouri*'s crew

The crew of the *Missouri* barely escaped with their lives.

Up in flames
Union supply ships were fired on from the city of Vicksburg

In 1863, the supply ship *Henry Clay* caught fire and sank during the bombardment of Vicksburg, Mississippi, by Union forces, during the Civil War.

Guns blazing

Many fierce naval battles were fought during the **Civil War** between the northern, Union, and southern, Confederate, states. In 1863, a fleet carrying arms and supplies to the Union army in the city of Vicksburg sailed up the Mississippi. Confederate forces lit enormous fires along the coast, which made the ships easy targets. Remarkably, only one ship, the *Henry Clay*, was destroyed by fire. The other ships landed successfully farther down the river and delivered their supplies.

HOT SPOTS
*On February 9, 1942, the luxurious ocean **liner** Normandie, was being refitted in New York to carry soldiers. A spark fell on a pile of life jackets, which quickly caught fire. Firefighters poured so much water on the burning ship that it sank!*

Harbor disasters

Some of the most serious shipwrecks have happened in the safety of harbors. Just when everyone thought nothing could go wrong, something terrible happened.

Roll over

In 1915, the liner *Eastland* was hired to take passengers on a picnic on Lake Michigan. The ship had recently been fitted with bigger lifeboats. By 7:00 A.M., 2,500 passengers were on board on the riverfront in Chicago. The weight of the people and the new lifeboats made the *Eastland* top-heavy. The ship suddenly rolled over, and more than 800 people drowned, even though the water was calm and only 20 feet (6 m) deep.

Lake Michigan

Chicago •

Desperate escape
People can be seen trying to get off the ship. But many people died, trapped below deck

Just as the *Eastland* was about to leave, hundreds of passengers rushed to one side of the deck to get a view of the river—and the ship capsized.

Tragic mistake

On March 6, 1987, the *Herald of Free Enterprise* **ferry** steamed out of Zeebrugge harbor in Belgium. The ship had big bow doors to allow cars to drive on and off. These doors were left open, and as the ferry picked up speed, the sea poured in. After only 90 seconds, the vessel filled with water and turned over on its side. Of the 539 passengers and crew on board, 193 drowned in one of the worst peacetime marine tragedies since the sinking of the *Titanic* in 1912.

HOT SPOTS

Ferry disasters are still happening. In 2006, more than 1,000 people died when the Egyptian ferry al-Salam Boccaccio 98 caught fire and sank in the Red Sea.

The *Herald of Free Enterprise* on its side as rescue ships took survivors to safety.

Trapped below

Many passengers were eating in the ship's restaurant when the accident happened

Open doors

The ship's doors should have been closed

Polluting wrecks

Modern shipwrecks brought a new peril—**pollution**. During the twentieth century, bigger and bigger **tankers** were built to carry oil. When they sank, the oil polluted the sea and shore for miles.

Alaska

NORTH AMERICA

Exxon Valdez wreck

Huge disaster

The *Exxon Valdez* was enormous: 1,000 feet (300 m) long, 165 feet (50 m) wide, and 90 feet (27 m) tall. On the night of March 24, 1989, it hit a reef off the coast of Alaska and millions of gallons of oil poured into the sea.

The *Exxon Valdez* oil spill caused the worst-ever sea pollution, killing about 250,000 sea birds, 2,800 sea otters, and 300 seals.

In 2004, a federal judge ordered Exxon to pay $4.5 billion in damages for the *Valdez* oil spill.

Area of oil spill
Stretched for more than 450 miles (750 km)

Amount leaked
Enough oil to fill 125 Olympic-sized swimming pools

Bad plans

In 1967, due to a navigational error, the **supertanker** *Torrey Canyon* struck a reef off the southwest coast of the UK. British planes tried bombing the tanker to make it sink before its oil leaked into the sea, but this plan did not work. Neither did the idea to burn the ship's leaking oil. The pollution killed sea life and ruined beaches for hundreds of miles around.

United Kingdom

Torrey Canyon oil spill •

HOT SPOTS

In 2002, the Prestige *oil tanker was wrecked off the Spanish coast. A year later, its oil was still polluting beaches hundreds of miles away.*

Crude oil

The *Torrey Canyon* was one of the world's first supertankers. It carried 132,000 tons of oil

This official picture, taken by the Royal Navy on March 3, 1967, shows the stern of the broken *Torrey Canyon* after it had struck Seven Stones Reef off Land's End.

Sea-slick

Leaking oil quickly spread along the Cornish and French coasts

Finding wrecks today

Throughout history, divers have tried to find wrecks and **salvage** treasure. Modern technology has made this work easier and less dangerous.

The submersible

One of the earliest uses of submarines was to find shipwrecks and salvage treasure. **Submersibles** and **bathyspheres** were among the early submarine models used for this purpose. Modern salvage ships are often semisubmersible, which means that a large part of the vessel is under water. They carry huge electric cranes to lift wrecks when they find them.

Going down
Strong lights are essential in deep water, where it is very dark and murky

The *Johnson Sea-link's* submersible was built in 1971 for deep-sea scientific research.

HOT SPOTS

After a collision on January 24, 1909, the RMS Republic *was wrecked off the coast of Nantucket, Massachusetts. Most of the passengers were rescued, but the gold it was carrying for the Czar of Russia sank with the ship. There have been many attempts to find the treasure, but without success.*

Rescued treasure

We explore wrecks not just for the value of their cargo. Ancient wrecks are like time capsules that give valuable clues about how people lived in the past. Underwater archaeologists uncover history's secrets by studying their finds in great detail. Divers also explore wrecks for fun. But diving to some wrecks is not allowed because they are of great historic importance or they are war graves.

Take a dive
Divers can spend months and sometimes years searching for a hidden wreck

Many divers risk their lives searching for long-lost ships, in the hope that they will learn more about the ship and how and why it sank.

Glossary

bathyspheres Strong, deep-sea diving vehicles that are lowered by a cable.

battleship A heavily armored warship, of the nineteenth and twentieth centuries.

brass Metal made by mixing copper and tin.

buoys Floating bells or lights that warn ships of danger.

cannons Large, heavy guns mounted on wheels, usually fired from a warship.

cargo Goods carried by a ship.

Civil War (1861–65) War fought in the U.S. between the northern and southern states.

civilians People not in the armed services or police force.

collision When two or more ships crash into each other.

crew People who work on a ship.

ferry Short-distance passenger ship.

fleet A group of ships sailing together under one commander.

galleons Large, three-masted sailing ships.

gunpowder An explosive used in guns to make them fire bullets.

harbor A sheltered port where ships are protected from bad weather.

hull The main body of a ship.

keel The main, long timber or steel support along the base of a ship.

lighthouse A tower on the shore with a light at the top to warn ships.

liner A large passenger ship, one of a group of similar ships owned by the same company or "line."

navigation Working out a position, and planning and following a route at sea.

New World A term used to describe North and South America. Also known as the Americas.

Pearl Harbor
A harbor on the island of Oahu, Hawaii, west of Honolulu, in the Pacific Ocean.

pollution The effect of poisonous or harmful substances on the environment or atmosphere.

porcelain Fine, hard china. The process of making porcelain was invented by the Chinese.

privateers Private individuals who hold an official government license to capture enemy merchant shipping.

reef Dangerous ridges of rock, sand or coral in the sea, on which ships are often wrecked.

rudder A device at the back of a ship used for steering.

running aground
When a ship becomes stranded on the seabed because the water is too shallow.

salvage To save ships or their cargo from destruction or loss at sea.

submersibles Small submarines that work underwater for short periods. They are designed to operate in deep water, below levels at which divers can work.

supertanker A very large tanker.

tankers Ships that carry liquids, such as oil.

Tudor Kings and queens from the same family who held the English throne from 1485 until 1603.

wreckers Thieves who stole the cargo of wrecked ships.

Index

Web sites

www.eastlanddisaster.org/summary.htm   Find out more about how a fun day out turned into a tragedy.

www.pirates-shipwrecks-treasure-diving.com/   All you need to know about hunting for shipwrecks.

www.en.wikipedia.org/wiki/Exxon_valdez_oil_spill   The full story of the Exxon Valdez disaster with lots of other links.

www.maryrose.org/   Take a tour of the Mary Rose Museum, explore the Mary Rose, and meet the crew.

www.lusitania.net/disaster.htm   A detailed breakdown of the Lusitania disaster, the rescue of survivors, and the recovery of bodies.